BOOK D
BASIC READING

GLENN McCRACKEN
New Castle, Pennsylvania
CHARLES C. WALCUTT
Queens College, Flushing, New York

J. B. LIPPINCOTT COMPANY
PHILADELPHIA, NEW YORK

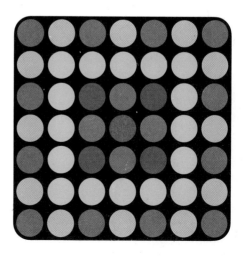

Copyright ©, 1975, 1969, 1966, 1963, by J. B. Lippincott Company
Printed in the United States of America
International Rights Reserved
ISBN-0-397-43547-9

CONTENTS

oi

join oil toil soil spoil loin noise moist
boil coin joint poise point noisy voice
foil hoist broil choice

oy

boy Roy oyster enjoy toy boyhood
joy royal Joyce annoy

The Shepherd Boy

There once was a shepherd boy who tended his sheep at the foot of a big hill. It was near a dark forest.

The soil there at the foot of the hill was good and moist. It made the grass nice and green. So the sheep enjoyed grazing all day.

But the shepherd boy was lonely.

So, one day, just for fun, the boy rushed down to the village. He called out in a loud voice, "Wolf, wolf!"

The boy made quite a noise.

All of the villagers came running to join the boy and to help protect his flock.

No one saw a wolf, but some of the villagers stayed with the boy for a long time.

The boy enjoyed this so much that the next day he tried the same thing.

Again, the villagers joined him to help. But there was no wolf and they were annoyed.

Shortly after this, a wolf really came out from the forest and started to worry the sheep.

The boy quickly ran to the village. He called out in a voice much louder than before, "Wolf, wolf!"

Over and over he called, "Wolf, wolf!" and he pointed to the forest. What a fuss the boy made!

But the shepherd boy had annoyed the villagers twice before. They did not want to be fooled again. So not one of them came out to join the boy. Not one of them came to his aid.

With no one to help protect the sheep, the wolf made a good meal of the boy's flock. The wolf went away licking his lips with loud, greedy noises.

The boy was angry and sad. When the boy went to the village, the wise man told him something to remember.

"Shepherd boy, now you see how important it is to tell the truth, not just now and then, but all the time."

The Milkweed Seed

The milkweed seed
Is not ripe
   to be freed,
When the pod
   is still green
And not grown.

When the pod
   becomes brown,
Then the seed
   will fly down
On a little cruise
   all its own.

—*Adele H. Seronde*

7

ew

drew grew crew strew threw chew
blew flew screw new dew stew
few pew mew

eau

beauty beautiful

The Deer and the Hunter

It was a nice clear morning in the forest. There was a little dew on the ground, but a new sun was rising over the trees.

A beautiful deer was drinking from a pool. As he drew up the water, he saw his reflection.

"Ah," said he, "few animals in the forest have such noble horns as mine. What beautiful antlers! I only wish I had legs more worthy to carry such a noble crown of antlers. It is a pity my legs grew so narrow and slim."

9

At that moment, a hunter blew his
horn. He aimed his arrow at the deer.

Away bounded the deer. With his
nimble legs he ran so fast that you
may say he almost flew.

The deer nearly got away from the
hunter. But not noticing where he was
going, he passed under a few trees
with low twigs. His beautiful antlers
got snarled up in them.

"Oh," cried the deer, "I hear the hunter coming, and I am stuck here by my antlers." He turned his antlers this way and that way. Finally, he worked his way free, just in time.

"I am lucky," he said. "I admired my antlers very much, but I almost got killed when they got stuck in the tree. It was my legs that helped me escape. It is true that we sometimes dislike what is most useful to us."

The Little Bird

Once I saw a little bird
   Come hop, hop, hop,
So I cried, "Little bird,
   Will you stop, stop, stop?"
And was going to the window
   To say, "How do you do?"
But he shook his little tail,
   And far away he flew.

—*Old Nursery Rhyme*

aw

saw law claw jaw paw hawk squaw
awning yawn awe shawl dawn lawn
yawning awful bawl crawl straw

au

saucer cause gauze pause haunt
haul Paul Paula fault author
launch because

caught taught daughter

Hopscotch

Paula Shaw liked to play hopscotch in front of her house. She had a wide, smooth cement pavement there. She marked out the game with colored crayons.

She used blue crayons, red crayons, yellow crayons, and orange crayons to color the squares. She drew the lines carefully. She said it took an awful lot of crayons to make the game look beautiful.

One Tuesday in June a young man with a banjo came by. He had a playful dog on a long rope. He paused to look

15

at Paula's game. "That's a beauty," he said.

Soon Paula saw a man coming with a huge mass of balloons floating above him in the blue sky. The playful dog barked and tried to reach the balloons. He jumped up and caught the strings in his teeth.

The balloon man bawled at the young man, "It's your fault!" He grabbed the dog's rope and got tangled in the strings of his balloons. A crowd gathered.

They pushed from the outside and caused the young man and the balloon man to step on Paula's beautiful game.

A few people in the crowd stepped on it too.

Paula saw her game being ruined, but she had an idea.

She caught the dog's rope in her hand. Paula ran up the street and under an awning. The balloon man had to follow because the dog's rope was tangled in the strings of his balloons. The young man ran after them.

The crowd followed because they had to see what happened. So they all moved away from the hopscotch game. Paula's idea had worked.

ph spells /f/

photograph telephone elephant nephew
pharmacy Philip pamphlet orphan
phonograph telegraph phantom Ralph
Phyllis autograph Joseph

ch spells /k/

character chemistry chemical chemist
chorus Christmas chrome school
scholar ache stomach echo scheme
schooner anchor orchestra mechanic

ch spells /sh/

Chicago machine chute Charlotte

A Funny Christmas Present

Philip Anderson lived on Spring Street in a small town called Andover. He was seven years old.

Philip had a little sister. Her name was Phyllis. Phyllis was five years old.

On Christmas morning Philip and Phyllis came running downstairs. They were very excited because they wanted

to see what was under the Christmas tree.

"I see something!" called Phyllis. "It is a toy elephant. It must be for me. And look at this pretty telephone. Now I can call you on the telephone, Mother."

Phyllis saw some other things that were for her, too—a phonograph that can play real records, a new dress, and some blocks.

Philip liked his presents, too. He got a chemistry set, an autograph book, a sled, and a nice warm coat.

"I can take my chemistry set to school," said Philip. "My teacher will show me how to use it."

Philip and his sister played with the presents all morning. Then, at twelve o'clock, Father said, "It is time for us to go to Grandmother and Grandfather Anderson's for Christmas dinner. Put on your coats and hats and boots."

On the way to Grandfather's house, the children saw what a pretty Christmas day it was. The lawns and trees were covered with sparkling snow. In front of one house they saw a big snowman.

Grandmother had a good Christmas dinner. There was turkey with chestnut dressing, fluffy mashed potatoes, brown gravy, ice cream, and other good things.

"I am so hungry," said Philip, "that I am going to eat all afternoon. Please let me eat and eat until I am stuffed."

"You must not eat too much," said Phyllis, "or you will get a stomach ache."

But Philip paid no attention to his sister. He just kept on eating and eating.

Later in the afternoon, Philip's Uncle Paul came to visit everybody at Grandmother's house. He saw that Philip was not feeling well. Poor Philip was sitting on the floor holding his stomach.

"What did you get for Christmas?" Uncle Paul asked Philip.

"Well," said Philip in a very sad voice, "I got a chemistry set, and an autograph book, a sled, a coat, AND A STOMACH ACHE!"

"Who gave you the chemistry set?" asked Uncle Paul.

"Mother," said Philip.

"And who gave you the autograph book?"

"Father."

"And the sled?"

"Grandmother and Grandfather."

"And the coat?"

"You gave me that," said Philip.

"Well, then," asked Uncle Paul, "who gave you the stomach ache?"

"Nobody," said Philip. "I gave it to myself. It was all my fault. Next Christmas I will not eat so much dinner. Then I will have only Christmas presents I like."

wr

wrap   wren   wrench   wring   wringer
wringing   wrist   wrong   write   writer
writing   wrote   wreath   wreck

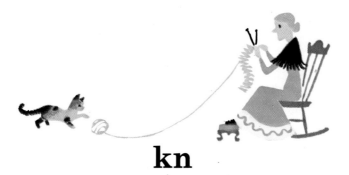

kn

knob   knot   knee   kneel   knit   knitted
knife   know   knew   known   knead
kneading   knack   knock   knocked
knocking

The Reading Lesson

It was a warm fall day. Leaves were just starting to tumble from the trees. There was a cool breeze blowing. It made the fallen leaves brush softly against each other on the ground.

It was not so cold that Ralph and Mary had to wrap up in winter coats and hats and knitted scarves. They just wore the red and white jackets that Aunt Alice had made for them.

It was the first day of school. Ralph and Mary were on their way. Mary was just going to start the third grade. She liked school very much. She knew how to read and write and spell and draw. She knew numbers and history.

Ralph had never been in school before. This was to be his first day in the first grade.

Mary saw that Ralph looked sad. "What is wrong, Ralph?" she asked. "You are going to school. When I was about to start the first grade, I was very happy. Does it make you sad?"

"Yes," said Ralph, "I do not think I am going to like school. Why must I know reading and writing and numbers? I do not want to be a magazine writer or a teacher when I grow up. I want to be a mechanic like Father or a salesman like Uncle Joseph. All I have to know is how to use tools like a hammer and wrench and screwdriver and how to sell things. I do not need reading and writing for that."

"But you are wrong, Ralph," said Mary. "You need reading and writing and numbers for almost everything. A salesman must be able to read his orders. He must add up his bills. He must sometimes write to his customers.

"A mechanic," said Mary, "must read directions for fixing cars."

"Suppose you wanted to be a painter," said Mary. "How can you know how much paint to mix if you cannot read the directions on a paint can? How can you know how long to let it dry? Or how many coats of paint a room needs?"

Just then the children passed a toy store with many toys in the window. "Look," said Ralph. "There is a toy car. I have been saving for one just like this one. I wonder how much it is."

"Well," said Mary. "There is a big card with writing on it. You can see

toys and the prices are beside each name. Now you see that there are many times when it is good to know how to read."

"Well," said Ralph, "what you are saying is true. Uncle Joseph gave me a model airplane kit for my birthday. I must know how to read before I can tell how to glue it together."

"But," said Mary, "you are wrong if you think that you only read when you need directions. Reading is fun, too.

"Sometimes you read just because you want to. Sometimes you read because you want to know what is happening in your town or city. You may want to read about your favorite baseball player in a newspaper or magazine or book."

"Yes," said Ralph, "I'd like to know all about Roberto Clemente. I think he was the best baseball player."

"Well," said Mary "after school today I will take you to the town library. I will show you where all the books about baseball are kept. If you want, you can even ask the librarian for a library card. Then when you know how to read, you can get all the books you want."

"Maybe I can find a book about machines and football and spaceships," said Ralph.

"I am sure you will find lots of books to read," said Mary. "I am going to look for *Robinson Crusoe.* That is a very exciting story."

Just then, Ralph and Mary came to the school. Ralph did not look sad any more. He wanted to meet his teacher and classmates.

Ralph told Mary, "I had my first lesson in reading today. But it was before I even started school. Now I want to know how to read. I think it will be fun to read books."

"I will see you after school today," said Mary, as she waved good-by to Ralph. "Yes," said Ralph, "and we will go to the library." He was smiling as he waved back to Mary.

Silent b

comb bomb limb climb dumb thumb
numb crumb plumber lamb debt
doubt

Silent l

talk talking walk walking sidewalk
stalk chalk folks calm palm half
calf solder could would should

Paul's Four Wishes

Once there was a little boy named Paul whose father liked to move from place to place. In place of staying calmly in one job, he made changes.

At first he was a plumber, and he was a good plumber. He could cut and fit pipes and solder copper tubes like an expert. But he used to walk up and down in the living room of their house and make plans for a change.

He said, "I am tired of being a plumber. I think I could do very well if I joined the Air Force. Perhaps with my skill as a plumber, I would make a good mechanic. Perhaps I could work on a big bomber."

So he joined the Air Force and was sent off to school to study all about airplanes. After a month, he came home on his first leave. It was in the middle of winter. He walked up and down in the living room, talking about his work at the Air Force School.

Paul asked, "Daddy, do they write on blackboards at your school?"

"Yes," said Paul's father, "they do. I doubt that you could find any better chalk or blackboards anywhere. They have green chalkboards and yellow chalk."

"Do you like it very much at the Air Force School?" asked Paul.

"Yes, but I get tired. My head gets numb from thinking so hard. And when I climb into my bed, I have figures and numbers whirling around in my brain. As a plumber, I knew just what to do. In the Air Force there are many things I do not know."

Well, Paul liked to copy his father. When his father went back to Air Force School after his leave, Paul decided that he, too, was tired of brain work. He pretended that his brain was numb from studying.

He said to himself, "I wish I could stop going to school. I wish I had nothing to eat but candy. I wish it would always be summer. I wish we had yellow chalk in school."

These were Paul's four wishes. They were not very sensible wishes, but Paul really didn't think very hard before he made them.

Paul was thinking about his wishes that evening at the dinner table. He and his mother were just eating the last crumbs of their dinner when his Uncle James dropped by. He had a huge bag under his arm.

"What have you there, Uncle James?" asked Paul.

"Well," said Uncle James, "today a strange thing happened to me. I was in my office after lunch. I had had a big lunch, and I must admit that I

dozed off for a minute or two. And while I was dozing there, I dreamed an odd dream.

"I dreamed that you, Paul, had made a wish that you could eat nothing but candy. So I decided to do a foolish thing. I went to the store and got the biggest box of chocolate candy I could find. Here it is!"

Uncle James unwrapped his package and placed a five-pound box of candy on the table.

Paul did not say it aloud, but he said to himself, "That is one of my wishes! Now I could eat nothing but candy if I really wanted to."

Just a week later, something very strange indeed happened. Paul's father telephoned long-distance. The next day he came up the sidewalk carrying a big bag over his shoulder.

He kissed Paul's mother and said, "We are going to move South. I have been moved to another air base. We shall have to pack up all the things in our house, climb into our car, and drive to our new home in Florida."

"But," said the mother, "that will take Paul out of school! How will Paul learn to read and write if we take him out of school?"

"Ah," said Paul, very surprised, "that is another of my wishes."

After some very busy days of packing and loading, the family drove off in their car. They drove out of the cold and the deep snow, down into the South. They drove across many states, until it became warm.

Paul saw his first palm tree. "Mother," he asked, "may I climb a palm tree?"

"You may try, but you will find that it does not have limbs like the trees at home up North. Its limbs point up, and they have sharp spines

on them. The leaves are not on twigs but on scratchy stalks. Only a monkey or an expert can climb a palm tree."

"And, anyhow," said his father, "most of the palm trees in Florida do not have coconuts up in their tops.

So why should you want to climb them?"

"Well," said Paul, "I should like to climb them. Then I should be able to say that I had climbed a palm tree when we return to the North."

Then Paul was suddenly very much surprised. "Why," he cried to himself, "that is still *another* one of my wishes! Here it is always summer."

So Paul had three of his four wishes granted in these strange ways. He was surprised again to find that life was very much the same even with three of his wishes granted.

If you are wondering about his last wish, this is what happened. Paul did not stay out of school very long. It was just a few days until the family got unpacked and settled in the new house.

And he was the most surprised of all to find that his new school in the South had green chalkboards and yellow chalk.

After that, Paul was a little bit careful about making wishes. You never can tell what will happen. And Paul still wonders what made his wishes all come true.

silent **g**

gnat gnats gnaw gnash gnashes sign
signboard reign foreign gnarl

silent **h**

John hour honor honest ghost ghastly
exhaust herb Thomas

silent **gh**

right night might sight light flight
fight fright slight sigh high thigh
bright straight
caught taught daughter

gh spells /**f**/

laugh laughter

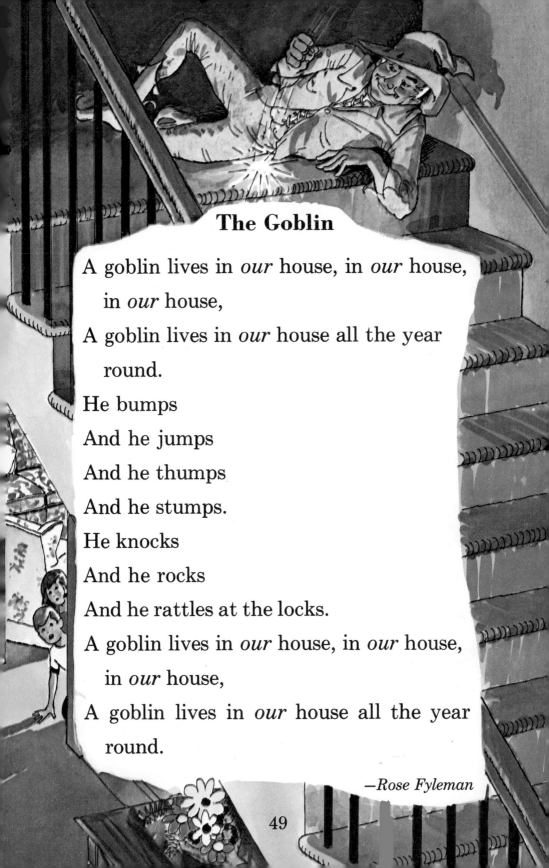

The Goblin

A goblin lives in *our* house, in *our* house,
   in *our* house,
A goblin lives in *our* house all the year
   round.
He bumps
And he jumps
And he thumps
And he stumps.
He knocks
And he rocks
And he rattles at the locks.
A goblin lives in *our* house, in *our* house,
   in *our* house,
A goblin lives in *our* house all the year
   round.

—*Rose Fyleman*

49

The Jack-O'-Lantern

Over in Cherry Valley lives a boy named John. John has a wagon, a little red wagon.

One bright day in the fall, John went up the road with his little red wagon. Up the road he walked until he saw a sign that said *Farmer Brown's Pumpkin Patch*. And beyond the sign John saw the huge pumpkin patch.

Now John was an honest boy. He was not the kind of bad boy who would steal a pumpkin. So he knocked on the farmhouse door. He asked if he might have a pumpkin from the farmer's pumpkin patch. John smiled brightly when Farmer Brown said he could have a pumpkin. John told Farmer Brown, "I want to make a jack-o'-lantern with

Big eyes to see
And teeth to bite,
So I can have fun
On Halloween night."

John went into the pumpkin patch and saw pumpkins, pumpkins, everywhere! The patch was dotted with them—big and little, green and yellow and orange.

John passed them by one after another. This one was too light, that one too dark, the next too large, the next too small.

But after a while John stopped. Before him was a pumpkin the color of gold. It was not too little, and not too big, but just right for a jack-o'-lantern.

"Oh, ho!" cried John. "Mister Pum-pumpkin, you are going home with me. You are going to have

Big eyes to see
And teeth to bite
So I can have fun
On Halloween night."

It took some tugging, but at last John got the pumpkin into his wagon. Then down the road he came, running like a runaway horse.

The wagon went bump, bump, bump!

The pumpkin went jump, jump, jump!

John was galloping along when all of a sudden the wagon ran into a big gnarled tree trunk. Away rolled the pumpkin down a steep, rocky hill. Over and over it tumbled until it struck a tree. Then plop! It flew into bits.

John cried, "I *must* have a pumpkin. I want to make a jack-o'-lantern

With eyes to see
And teeth to bite,
So I can have fun
On Halloween night."

And up the road he went again with his little red wagon.

John found another pumpkin the color of gold, not too little, not too big, but just right. He tugged until he got it into his wagon. Then down the road he came running as fast as before.

    The wagon went bump, bump, bump!

    The pumpkin went jump, jump, jump!

John went clip-clopping along. In a vegetable patch at the side of the road, he caught sight of a rabbit. The rabbit was gnawing on a carrot.

To see the rabbit better, John left
the wagon and climbed over the wall.
When he came back, a cow was eating
his pumpkin. The big white seeds lay
scattered all over the ground.

John sighed, "I *must* have a
pumpkin. I want to make a
jack-o'-lantern

> With eyes to see
> And teeth to bite,
> So I can have fun
> On Halloween night."

And up the high hill he went again with his little red wagon.

John found another pumpkin the color of gold, not too little, not too big, but just right. He tugged until he got it into his wagon. Then down the road he came running as fast as ever.

The wagon went bump, bump, bump!

The pumpkin went jump, jump, jump!

John ran past the big gnarled tree trunk, clippity-clop. He passed the

cow. He passed the vegetable patch where the rabbit was gnawing a carrot. He would not stop for anything. He just ran on and on until he was at home.

John laughed and said, "Now I can make a jack-o'-lantern, a funny one." Then he looked in his wagon. No pumpkin there! John had lost the pumpkin. It had jumped out of the wagon.

John sighed, "I *must* have a pumpkin. I want to make a jack-o'-lantern

With eyes to see
And teeth to bite,
So I can have fun
On Halloween night."

"Polly! Polly!" John called to his sister. "Will you go high up the hill to the pumpkin patch with me? I want you to help me get a pumpkin."

Polly was willing. So up the road they both went with the little red wagon.

They found a pumpkin the color of gold, not too little, not too big, but just right. They boosted it into the wagon. Then down the road they came walking—cl-op, cl-op. All the way home they walked very slowly, with Polly holding on to the pumpkin.

The wagon did not bump, bump, bump!

The pumpkin did not jump, jump, jump!

It jogged along merrily over the weeds and stones, and right up to the doorstep in John's back yard.

Then, while Polly made a Halloween ghost from an old sheet, John made a jack-o'-lantern.

He cut two eyes and a three-cornered nose. Then he cut a mouth so big that it could have eaten a huge pie all at once.

It was night when John finished, and the hour was late. John put the jack-o'-lantern on the porch post with a red candle inside. Its eyes, round as cart wheels, glowed like fire in the dark. Its mouth showed rows of long, sharp teeth.

The cat was so frightened she ran under the porch. The puppy backed away and barked and barked.

"Polly!" called John, laughing. "Polly, come out! My jack-o'-lantern
Has eyes to see
And teeth to bite.
Come and have fun,
It's Halloween night."

The Moon

The moon
The moon
So white
So cool
Will soon
So soon
Alight
In the pool
  Dark pool
    Of night.

—*Adele H. Seronde*

ea spells short e

thread head dead read ready dread
dreadful lead bread spread deaf
breast health healthy wealthy meant
feather leather weather heavy sweat
breath meadow pleasant

ea spells long a

break breaks breaking daybreak great
greater steak beefsteak

ear spells /er/

learn search earth heard pearl
earn early

ear spells /air/

bear pear wear tear tearing

ear spells /ar/

heart hearth

A Hearty Meal

Oh, bread and meat
Are good to eat
  With steak
    And pickled pear,

Add heavy cream
And every seam
  Will break
    Or burst
      Or tear!

—*Adele H. Seronde*

The Grizzly Bear

Have you ever read or heard a story about a grizzly bear? If so, you no doubt know that these great big animals sleep all winter long. If you saw one in his cave, you might think he was dead. But he is really very much alive. As soon as the cold weather passes and the pleasant spring weather comes, he wakes up.

Here is a story about a great, big, healthy grizzly bear who lived in the north woods.

It was just daybreak on the first day of spring. The grizzly bear woke up from his long winter sleep.

"That was a pleasant nap," he said, yawning, "but I am glad the good weather has returned."

Then the grizzly bear felt his great big stomach. It was quite empty. "Oh, how hungry I am," he said. He found a bit of bread in his cave and gobbled it up. But you know that a scrap of bread certainly was not going to fill that great stomach.

So out of his cave into the bright sunlight went the grizzly bear to search for some food. He walked out of the forest, past a running brook, and across a green meadow.

Suddenly he stopped and twitched his nose. Something good was being cooked in the cabin where the game warden lived.

The grizzly bear crept to the window and saw the warden's wife getting a meal ready. Spread out on

the table near her was a big loaf of
brown bread and some raw beefsteak.
The beefsteak was all red and juicy.

The grizzly bear felt the gnawing
of hunger in his great stomach, and
his mouth began to water. "That
beefsteak looks mighty good," he said
to himself.

The game warden's wife was a bit deaf, and so she had not heard the bear approaching. She turned around and saw his great head at the window. She let out a dreadful scream and ran out the back door of the cabin.

The grizzly bear did not even have to break the door down to enter the cabin. He just walked straight in and grabbed the juicy beefsteak and the brown bread in his mouth. The game

warden's wife, who was hiding behind
a tree, watched the bear hurry away.
Away he ran to eat the steak and
bread in peace in his cave.

Looking very proud, the grizzly bear
ran across the green meadow. He came
to the running brook. As he ran on
the board lying across the brook, he
looked down. He saw his own
reflection in the water.

Thinking it was another grizzly bear with another meal of bread and beefsteak, he made up his mind to have that also. He meant just to snarl and growl, but as he opened his mouth, the beefsteak and bread fell out and dropped into the water.

The grizzly bear then knew that he had lost the real meat and bread by grasping at the reflection. Sadly he walked away, for he had learned his lesson.

ie spells long e

chief thief thieves brief field priest
yield shield grief grieve

cities kitties daisies stories candies
ponies ladies Annie pennies empties
fifties puppies sixties carries berries
copies pansies bunnies lilies Bessie

believe fierce shriek belief niece relief
pierce achieve piece

ei spells long e

receive perceive conceive ceiling
either neither

Blue Flower

There once was a little Indian girl named Blue Flower. Blue Flower was the niece of the chief of the tribe. His name was Sky Chief.

Blue Flower knew that her Uncle Sky Chief was the bravest and wisest of the Indians in the tribe. He was fierce in battle. He would lead his men to battle with wild yells and shrieks. But Blue Flower knew that Sky Chief was also a gentle man. She loved him dearly.

Blue Flower, and all the other Indians in her tribe, believed that there was a strange and beautiful bird called a thunderbird. They believed that this bird made thunder.

One day Blue Flower went to the meadow near her wigwam. She wanted to see the thunderbird.

She looked everywhere. She looked
in trees and bushes. She looked in
fields of clover and in fields of daisies.
She saw many pretty birds in the
fields and trees. But she could not
find a thunderbird.

Blue Flower was disappointed.

"I'll ask Sky Chief about the
thunderbird," said Blue Flower. "He
will know all about it."

Blue Flower went to Sky Chief's wigwam. Sky Chief had the biggest wigwam with the highest ceiling.

There were shields and pieces of gold and silver along the walls. Indian beads hung from the ceiling.

Sky Chief sat in the center. He was wearing his beautiful feather headdress. He did not look fierce at all.

"What do you wish, my niece?" asked Sky Chief.

"I want to see the thunderbird," said Blue Flower.

Sky Chief laughed. "You cannot see the thunderbird," he said. "The thunderbird lives very high in the sky. But you know that a thunderbird is passing by when you hear a loud clap of thunder."

"Oh," said Blue Flower, "if I cannot see the thunderbird, I can at least listen for him."

Blue Flower always listened closely for the thunder. Sometimes she said she could hear a great flapping of a bird's wings before the thunder.

Do you boys and girls believe in
a thunderbird? Have you ever heard
him?

ei spells long a

reins   reindeer   veil   vein   reign

eigh spells long a

neigh   sleigh   freight   eight   eighteen
eighty   weigh   weight   neighbor

ey spells long a

they   grey   whey   prey

The Adventure of Puffy and Tubby

Once upon a time, in the reign of King Cole, a family of silly frogs lived by a leafy pond. The leaves were big lilies that floated on the water. They were good to sit on in the sun, and to hide under.

The frogs could lie in the water with their chins resting on the lily pads. Their heads were the same color as the lily pads. They could not be seen by passing birds of prey—like herons, cranes, and even kingfishers. These big birds of prey greatly enjoy eating little frogs.

One day in the summer, the sun was high and hot and beating straight down on the pond. The silly family of frogs decided that they were tired of their leafy pond. They believed that they would travel over the hill to look for a bigger pond with more shade.

They also believed that while they were on their way they could see the world.

Because they had lived by their leafy pond for eight years, they had a house full of furniture and dishes. They also had many kinds of clothing to wear when they were not swimming in the leafy pond or resting on a lily pad.

"How," asked one little frog named Puffy, "are we going to move our property over the high hill? It will make a great load of freight that will weigh a great deal. It will be much too heavy for us to carry."

Just then, there was a loud sound on the road beside the pond. It was the neighing of a grey horse named Jason, who belonged to Farmer Jones. The farmer was a neighbor of the frog family. That is, the frogs said he was their neighbor. Farmer Jones did not say anything about the frogs because he was not interested in frogs.

When he heard the neighing of the horse, the little frog named Puffy said, "Perhaps we could hire Farmer Jones to take our property over the hill in his wagon. It would make a great load of freight!"

His father whose name was Boomer was very big. Boomer said, "Puffy, what would we use to pay Farmer Jones for his trouble of hauling this great load of freight? And anyway, it will weigh so much that Farmer Jones's horse, Jason, will not be able to pull it. Farmer Jones will slap the reins and shout 'Giddap!' but Jason will just stand still and neigh."

"Maybe if we wait until winter, we can put our property on a sleigh. Then Jason can pull it up over the great hill," said Puffy.

Boomer said, "Perhaps a sleigh would do better, but winter is a long time from now. Why don't you start up the hill with your brother Tubby? It would be pleasant to walk in the woods in the fine summer weather. You could surely climb as far as you wanted to, even halfway to the top of the great hill."

So Puffy and Tubby asked their mother to pack a lunch for them in a knapsack. She put watercress, pickled flies, and salted mosquitoes in the knapsack. Puffy took the knapsack for the first turn. The two little frogs started off past the trees and up the hill.

The weeds seemed as tall as hedges to them, and the ferns might have been palm trees. Stones that a boy might step or skip over looked like great boulders that would weigh many tons.

Presently they heard the sound of a bell. "Ah," said Puffy, "hear the bell ringing. Do you think it is a train, or a great church, or perhaps a clock in a big city?"

Just then the bell sounded again, very close to them this time, and there was a sniffing and a snuffling noise. And then the bell went "CLANG, CL-A-A-NN-NG, and KER-KLUNNNK," right close to their ears! Then the light of the sky was shut out by a huge form that towered over them. A grey thing came down closer and closer to the two

frightened frogs, and it went "SNUFF SNORT WHUFFLE WHOOSH."

The poor frogs did not know that it was only Farmer Jones's cow. They just sat there, trying to hide. Then the cow walked away, because cows do not eat frogs.

But Tubby and Puffy hopped back down the hill as fast as they could hop, knapsack and all.

That night all the silly frogs had a family conference. They decided that their leafy pond was as big as they needed. They also agreed that it was not safe to go mountain climbing in that part of the country.

The Giant's Eye

If I
Could fly high
As a giant's eye
I should spy
The wide sea
From the sky!
The clouds would lie under
Me, filling with thunder
And the wind
Would ride
Crying
By!

—Adele H. Seronde

School Under the Trees

(A Story About **Ough**)

Freddie Applegate was seven years old and in the first grade. One afternoon in May he came home from school very excited. He skipped down the street. When he got to his house, he ran across the lawn. Then he raced up the steps in two jumps. On the porch, his little sister, Judy, was playing in the sun.

Suddenly Freddie stopped. He looked at Judy without saying anything. Then he said, "I am going to have a schoolroom."

"What do you want with a schoolroom?" asked Judy.

"I want to be a teacher this afternoon," said Freddie. "I want some children who can learn how to read. I want to give a reading lesson."

"But why today?" asked Judy. "You have been having reading lessons all year, haven't you? That's all I hear about at dinner, most of the time."

"Today," said Freddie in an important tone, "I have learned some very interesting things in school. Now I want to teach them to somebody else. So I will run across the yard and call Jimmy Henderson and Alfie Sparks. I want them to come over to my school."

"May I be a pupil?" asked Judy.

"Of course you can. And you can make Jimmy and Alfie pay attention and not make any noise. You can be at the head of the class, too. You are learning to read already."

"I like that," called Judy, as she watched Freddie run across the big yard toward Jimmy Henderson's house.

As soon as he came back, Freddie said to himself, "I have it!"

He ran into his house. He went down
into the cellar where he made a great
commotion. When he came back up,
he was carrying a load of freight.
He had an old blackboard, some
chalk, and a handful of rags. He went
back down again and returned with
eight boards and two chairs.

He put the eight boards down on the grass. They made a large square. Inside the square he placed the two chairs. Then he said, "Oh, I have forgotten Judy," and he ran down into the cellar once more. When he returned, he was carrying a little stool which he placed beside the chairs. On the other side of the square he set up his blackboard. Just then Judy came back with Jimmy Henderson and Alfie Sparks.

"Hi, Jimmy; hi, Alfie; have a seat in my schoolroom. I am going to

teach you some re—mark—able facts about our language."

"What are you going to teach us?" asked Jimmy.

"Next year," said Freddie, "I'll be eight years old. I will be finishing the second grade, and I may have a great school of my own in the afternoons. I will teach all the children in the neighborhood."

Alfie said, "I know how to read. I know all the letters. I can even spell *cat*—c-a-t."

"Ah, yes, of course you can spell *cat*. But let's give you a harder word. Can you spell *muff?*"

Alfie said, "M-u-f-f spells *muff*. That's easy, too."

"All right. Now listen closely. What do you spell if you put a *t* in place of the *m* in *muff?*" asked Freddie.

Alfie laughed. "That is easy too. My steak was t-u-f-f, *tuff*." Alfie looked as if he knew he was smart.

"No. You're wrong. T-o-u-g-h spells *tough,* but it rhymes with *muff.*"

Freddie took his piece of chalk and wrote—

t o u g h

on the blackboard. "Did you know that gh can sound like f? Words ending in o-u-g-h can rhyme with *muff*. Here are some other words that rhyme with *muff*—" and he wrote these words on his blackboard—

r o u g h   e n o u g h

Alfie read them, making them rhyme with *muff*.

"Now," said Freddie, "it gets harder. Jimmy, did you know that words ending in o-u-g-h sometimes can rhyme with *off*? Let me hear you read—"

c o u g h

"Well," said Jimmy, "it must be *cough*. Is that really the way you spell it?"

"Right. Now, do you know what this is?"—And he wrote—

t r o u g h

on his blackboard. "It still rhymes with *off*."

Alfie said, "*Trough,* but what's a *trough,* Freddie?"

"A *trough,*" answered Freddie, "is a V-shaped little ditch. Water would

run in a *trough*. Or it is a wooden box for animals' food, like this . . ." and he drew it on the blackboard.

Alfie and Jimmy laughed. They were becoming interested in the lesson.

Then Jimmy asked, "What else can you spell with o-u-g-h?" He hoped Freddie would draw some other funny pictures.

"Next we make an o-u-g-h ending rhyme with *so*, just like *o*. Read—

d o u g h

Jimmy said, "*Dough*. Is that what bread is before it is baked?"

"Yes, very good. And now you can read—but let Alfie have his turn." And on the board Freddie wrote—

t h o u g h   a l t h o u g h

d o u g h n u t

"Now, Jimmy, there is one more hard one for you. We make this rhyme with *cow*. Then let's put a *b* in front of it—" and on the board he wrote—

b o u g h

"See what it says?"

"Yes," said Jimmy, "*bough*. Is it like a dog barking?"

"It's the limb of a tree. A *bough*."

"And now, there is still one more. Here it rhymes with *to;* it says *oo* like the *oo* in *food;* and suppose we put *thr* before it—" and he wrote—

t h r o u g h

"My turn," said Alfie. "It's *through*. I walked *through* the woods."

"Now!" said Freddie. "There is still one more kind of *ough* word. We can put a *t* on *bough*. We make a word that tells what you did when you paid money for something."

"I know," said Jimmy. *"Bought!"*

"Yes," said the teacher, and he wrote on the board—

b o u g h t   o u g h t

t h o u g h t

Freddie erased the blackboard and made a list of the words this way—with the sounds on the left, and the words on the right. Alfie and Jimmy took turns saying the words as Freddie wrote them with his chalk:

ough

muff enough That's enough soup.
      rough That's a rough sea.

off   cough A cold makes you cough.
      trough Pigs eat from a trough.

awt   ought I ought to be careful.
      thought He thought about it.
      bought He bought a pencil.

so dough Mother kneaded the dough.
      though I'll go, though it's late.

cow bough The bird sat on a bough.
too through I can see through it.

As Freddie pointed to the last word on the blackboard, he heard a loud noise. The two boys jumped up from their seats. The sound was thunder; and suddenly it had begun to rain.

"Let's go and play in my house. I have a good new game," said Jimmy to Freddie and Alfie.

"That sounds like fun," said Freddie. "I'll race the two of you."

And the three boys raced across the yard to Jimmy's house, leaving the schoolroom alone in the rain.

The Three Bears

Once upon a time there were three brown bears. They lived in a pretty house in the forest.

One of the bears was very big. He was the father. Then there was a middle-sized bear. She was the mother. One bear was very small. He was the baby.

The bears had three chairs in their house. One chair was big and strong. Father Bear sat in it. One chair was middle-sized. It was for Mother Bear. One chair was little. It was just the right size for Baby Bear.

The bears had three beds in their house. One was a big hard bed. Father Bear slept in it. One bed was not so big and not so hard. Mother Bear slept in it. Then there was a tiny soft bed for Baby Bear.

One day Mother Bear made a pot of porridge. At supper time she took

it off the stove. It was so hot it
was steaming.

She filled a large bowl with
porridge. It was for Father Bear's
supper. Then she put some porridge
into a middle-sized bowl for herself.
And she put a small cupful of

porridge into a little bowl. It was for Baby Bear's supper.

Father Bear tasted his porridge. It was much too hot to eat. So he said, "We will go for a walk in the soft snow. When we come back, our supper will be cool enough to eat."

While the bears were gone, a little girl came to the house where the bears lived. Her name was Goldilocks. She had pretty golden yellow hair.

Goldilocks looked in a window to see who lived in the house. She saw no one. Then Goldilocks went to the door. It was not locked; so she went in.

Goldilocks saw the bowls of porridge on the table. She started to eat some from the big bowl. It was too hot. She tried the middle-sized bowl. It was too hot, too.

Then she tasted the porridge in the little bowl. It was just right so Goldilocks ate all of it.

Goldilocks was very tired. She had
walked far from home and did not
know the way back. "I will sit down
and rest a while," she said.

She sat down in the big chair. It
was too big and too hard. She sat
in the middle-sized chair. It was too
hard, too. Then she tried the little
chair. It was just right.

But a funny thing happened. That chair was not big enough to hold Goldilocks. It broke into little pieces.

Goldilocks looked at the three beds. "I will rest in the big one," she said. But the big bed was too hard. She climbed into the middle-sized bed. It was too hard. She tried the little bed. It was just right. Goldilocks lay down in it and fell fast asleep.

After a while, the bears came back from their walk. "Now we will eat our supper," said Father Bear. Then he saw a spoon in his big bowl. "Who ate some of my porridge?" he called.

Mother Bear saw a spoon in her bowl, too. "Who ate some of my porridge?" she asked.

Then Baby Bear looked into his bowl. "Who has been eating my porridge?" cried Baby Bear. "Who ate it all up?"

The bears looked at their chairs. "Who has been sitting in my chair?" asked Father Bear in an angry voice. "And who has been sitting in my chair?" called Mother Bear. "Who has been sitting in my chair?" cried Baby Bear. "Who broke it all to pieces?"

By this time all three of the bears
were very angry. They began looking
to see who might be in their house.
At last they looked in their bedroom.

"Someone has been in my bed,"
said Father Bear. "And someone has
been in my bed," called Mother Bear.
"Someone has been in my bed," cried
Baby Bear, "and there she is now."

Goldilocks opened her eyes and took one look at the angry bears. Then she jumped out of the bed and ran to a window. She pushed open the window and climbed through it. The last thing the bears saw was Goldilocks running through the snow.

Goldilocks did not look back. She ran as fast as she could go until she got home.

The Three Little Pigs

Once there was an old pig who had three little pigs. She could not find enough food for all three pigs. So she sent them out into the world to look after themselves.

The little pigs traveled until they were far from home.

One day the first little pig met a man carrying a bundle of straw. "Please, Mr. Man," he said, "give me some straw so I can build myself a house."

The man gave the first little pig some straw, and he built a fine straw house.

The second little pig met a man carrying a bundle of sticks. "Please, Mr. Man, give me some sticks so I can build myself a house," said the pig. The man gave him the sticks and he built himself a pretty house.

The third little pig met a man with a load of bricks. He said, "Please, Mr. Man, give me some bricks so I can build myself a house." The man gave him the bricks, and he built a house with them.

Not long after this a wolf came to
the house that was made of straw.
"Little Pig," he said, "let me come
in."

"No, no!" said the little pig. "Not
by the hair of my chinny-chin-chin."

"Then I'll huff and I'll puff, and
I'll blow your house down!" said the
wolf. So he huffed and he puffed and
he blew the house down. The little
pig ran as fast as he could down the
road. He came to his brother's house
which was made of sticks. He knocked
on the door. His brother let him in.

Along came the wolf. He said, "Little Pig, let me come in."

"No, no!" said the second little pig. "Not by the hair of my chinny-chin-chin."

"Then I'll huff and I'll puff, and I'll blow your house down," said the wolf. So he huffed and puffed and puffed and huffed, and at last he

blew the house down. The two little pigs ran down the road as fast as they could.

At last they came to their brother's brick house. Their brother let them in.

The wolf came and said, "Little Pig, Little Pig, let me come in your house."

"No, no!" said the third little Pig. "Not by the hair of my chinny-chin-chin."

"Then I'll huff and I'll puff, and I'll blow your house down," said the wolf.

The wolf huffed and puffed and puffed and huffed, but the house did not fall down.

When he found he could not blow the house down, he said, "Little Pig, I know where there is a field of nice turnips."

"Where?" said the little pig.

"In Mr. Smith's field," said the wolf. "Tomorrow morning we will go together and get some for dinner."

"Very well," said the little pig. "What time shall I be ready to go?"

"Six o'clock," said the wolf.

The little pig got up at five. He went to get the turnips and was back home again before six.

When the wolf came at six o'clock, he said, "Little Pig, are you ready?"

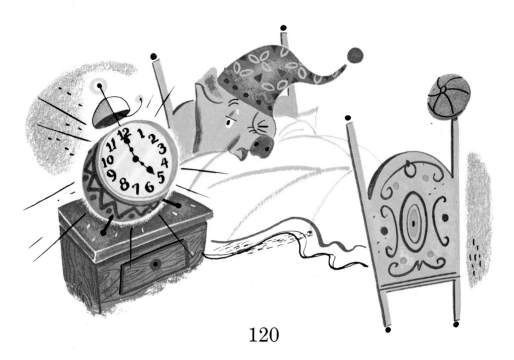

"Ready!" said the little pig. "I got the turnips and am back home again. What a nice potful I have for dinner."

The wolf was very angry. Then he began to think of how he could catch the little pig another day. He said, "Little Pig, I know where there is a nice apple tree."

"Where?" said the pig.

"Down at the Drake farm," said the wolf. "I will come for you at five o'clock tomorrow morning. We will go together and get some apples."

The next morning the pig got up at four o'clock and went to the apple tree. But the wolf thought the pig would go early, and he went soon after four.

122

The little pig was still in the tree
when the wolf got there. "Little Pig,"
said the wolf, "why are you here
before me? Are they nice apples?"

"Yes, very nice," said the pig. "I
will throw one down to you." He
threw an apple very far. While the
wolf was going to get it, the pig ran
home.

The next day the wolf came again. "Today," he said to himself, "I will have the third little pig for dinner. I know how to catch him now."

When the wolf came to the little brick house, he called in to the little pig, "Little Pig, let me come in."

"No, no!" said the little pig. "Not by the hair of my chinny-chin-chin."

Now the wolf was very angry indeed. He said, "I know how to get you now. I will come down your chimney and eat you." And then he did start to climb down the chimney.

The third little pig and his brothers had to think fast. And they did. There was a big pot of water on the fire just under the chimney. They made a big blazing fire to get the water very hot. Then they took the lid off the pot.

When the wolf came down the chimney, he fell into the pot. The water was so hot that the wolf howled and leaped out the chimney and they never saw him again.

The three little pigs lived happily ever after. The third little pig and the first and second little pigs had learned a lesson.

Robbie Rabbit

Once there were four little rabbits. Their names were Rose Rabbit, Roger Rabbit, Ralph Rabbit, and Robbie Rabbit. They lived with their mother in a house near a big forest.

One day Mrs. Rabbit said to her children, "I am going to visit Mrs. Bird. You may play while I am gone."

"But do not get your nice clean clothes dirty. Your clothes are old. But they are very clean. You must keep them that way."

Then Mrs. Rabbit took a basket and her umbrella and went to see Mrs. Bird.

Rose Rabbit, Roger Rabbit, and Ralph Rabbit were good little bunnies. They washed their hands and faces. They kept their clothes very, very clean. But Robbie Rabbit was naughty. He went down the dusty road. He climbed up on a big rock. And then he saw some big ripe tomatoes.

Robbie said to himself, "I will go and get a big tomato. I am hungry." He took a bite out of one tomato. It was good. Then he went to get some more tomatoes. But he did not see a stone in the way. He tripped on it, and down he fell! He fell right on top of all the tomatoes!

"Oh, oh, what shall I do?" said Robbie Rabbit. "My clothes are all dirty. I am so naughty. Mother will not be happy."

Robbie Rabbit went home. His brothers and sister laughed and laughed when they saw him.

Then Mrs. Rabbit came home. She saw Robbie Rabbit. "You are a naughty rabbit," she said. "Now you must put on your new Sunday suit. Your old clothes are all dirty."

Mrs. Rabbit scrubbed and scrubbed Robbie Rabbit. She scrubbed his face. She scrubbed his hands, and she even scrubbed his ears! Then Robbie Rabbit put on his new Sunday suit.

"Be careful, now," said Mrs. Rabbit. "You must not get your Sunday clothes dirty. You do not have any other clothes. Be careful."

Robbie looked at his new suit. "My, it is beautiful," he said. "I will be careful. I do not want to get it dirty. I will not go out to play."

So Robbie Rabbit did not go out to play. He watched his brothers playing. He watched his sister playing. But he stayed at home in his new Sunday suit.

"What shall I do now?" said Robbie Rabbit. "I cannot go out to play. I will stay here and help Mother."

So Robbie Rabbit swept the floor. He picked up all his toys. He even made his bed.

"Now I am a good little rabbit," he said.

Suddenly there was a knock on the door. Robbie Rabbit went to see who it was. It was Mrs. Bird.

"My, what a clean little rabbit you are," she said.

"Thank you," said Robbie Rabbit. "Do you want to see Mother?"

"No," said Mrs. Bird. "I want her to have these blueberries. Will you give them to her?"

"Yes," said Robbie Rabbit. "Goodby."

Robbie Rabbit took the blueberries to his mother.

"Mrs. Bird sent these to you," he said.

"Oh, how nice," said Mrs. Rabbit. "Now I can make a blueberry pie."

"Oh, yes," said Robbie Rabbit, "a big blueberry pie!"

"You can go out to play now, Robbie," said Mrs. Rabbit.

Robbie did not want to play. He was afraid that he would get his new Sunday suit dirty. So he sat by the window and watched his brothers and sister.

Soon he could smell the blueberry pie. "Hmm," he said. "I can hardly wait until we can eat the blueberry pie!"

Robbie went into the kitchen. On the table he saw the beautiful blueberry pie.

"I will climb up on the table. I want to see if the pie is cool," he said.

So up he climbed. But he did not see the rolling pin! He rolled over the rolling pin—right into the blueberry pie!

Mrs. Rabbit ran into the kitchen. "You are a naughty rabbit," said Mother Rabbit. "You must go to bed. Your new Sunday suit is dirty! I have more berries. I will make another pie. But you cannot have any."

Then she put Robbie Rabbit to bed.

Rose Rabbit, Roger Rabbit, and Ralph Rabbit were good little rabbits. They each had two pieces of blueberry pie. But Robbie Rabbit didn't have any pie at all.

Phoneme-grapheme Sequence in Books A — D

Book A

Sound	Page	Sound	Page	Sound	Page
short a	1	p	12	hard g	29
n	2	short i	15	hard c	32
r	3	s	18	h	36
d	5	short o	20	f	39
short u	7	t	22		
m	9	short e	25		

Book B

Sound	Page	Sound	Page	Sound	Page
ar	1	le	34	ai	58
er	5	k	37	long i, ie	64
ed	6	ck	39	ir	65
w	9	nk	41	long o	71
aw	19	signal e	44	ore, or	72
ow(cow)	24	a(care)	45	oa	78
l	26	long a	46	oe	78
ll	27	long e,ee	50	j	82
b	33	ea	54	v	87

Book C

Sound	Page	Sound	Page	Sound	Page
sh	1	-ing	33–38	dg,dge	89
ch,tch	5	-ed	44–47	-tion,-sion	97
th	8	er as er	52	oo(cook)	102
wh	14	ar as er	53	oo(food)	102
qu	17	ir,or,ur as er	54	ow(snow)	115
x	18	-y,-ay	64	ow(cow)	118
y	19	-ey	64	ou	119
z	20	soft c	75	long u	130
ng	26	soft g	88	ue,ui	130

Book D

Sound	Page	Sound	Page	Sound	Page
oi	1	kn	26	ea as long a	62
oy	1	silent b	36	ear	62
ew,eau	8	silent l	36	ie as long e	72
aw,au	14	silent g	48	ei as long e	72
ph as f	18	silent h	48	ei as long a	78
hard ch	18	silent gh	48	eigh as long a	78
ch as sh	18	gh as f	48	ey as long a	78
wr	26	ea as short e	62	ough	101

Acknowledgments

Illustrations: Ann Atene, Bill Hamilton, Helen Hamilton, Gisela Jordan, Tom King, Carol Kitzmiller, Roland V. Shutts, Edward John Smith, Barbara B. Werner, George Wilde.
Cover design: Phil Rath.